RAISING JUSTICE

Lessons Learned Through Motherhood

DORIS JACKSON SHAZIER

Edited By:
Name of Editor

Printed By:
Company Name

Printed in the United States of America

First Printing Edition, 2024

ISBN 0-0000000-0-0

Dedication

This book is dedicated to the child born with both eyes open. Justice, I remember you being placed on my chest and you looking me square in the eyes and then around the room. Aware and alert from the beginning. It has been a joy living, learning and growing with you. A part of me knew you when you were forming and I knew you would grow to honor your name. The following pages document the experiences in which I have learned from you. You are the daughter of my dreams. I love you. You are enough today, tomorrow and always.

This book is written by me, Inspired By You and definitely orchestrated by God.

To the wonderful men in my life, my doting husband, Deon, who has been by my side in raising our children. My three sons, Deon, Dorian & Davion. You all are so important to the story of my life. I love you;

This book is also dedicated to my mother's along the way.

My grandmother, Sandra Jackson. Thank you for being not only a grandmother but a mom. Caring, protective and reliable. You have always been there when I needed you. The older I get, the more I appreciate all that you have done for me. I love you so much.

My mother, Octavia Thomas-Clark, who I have come to know better through motherhood. You are loved and appreciated. I appreciate your courage to do what some would not have done. All things work together for our good, and God takes our pieces to make us whole. I love you.

My God-mother, Artesta Lewis. I thank God for sending you into my life. There was so much more for me to learn. You entered my life in a time when I needed the type of mother you are. You helped me develop so much spiritually. I love you.

My "Grandma Gailey" Gail Youmans. Thanks for stepping in as a friend, confidant and mother figure during my early stages of motherhood and beyond. You welcomed me into your family and have loved my growing family as your own.

Contents

CHAPTER ONE

Fate and Faith

"You know, if you named that baby, you wouldn't be able to do what you are thinking about doing."

Fate and faith are intricately linked, like a child nestled within a mother's womb. Our faith is much similar to a hopeful child trusting in their mother's guidance, and motherhood has only served to strengthen this belief in me.

When I look back, this journey has been a spiritual one. I vividly recall the day when I discovered that she was *still* there, defying all odds. Yes, *still* there, her heartbeat connected to mine. It had all begun with an unexpected rendezvous of September. The days that were once filled with promise had transformed into a sour memory overnight. The morning after our encounter, the guy revealed his true character. Fortunately, I made up my mind then and there to sever all ties with him. Little did I know that this decision to end the relationship would only be short-lived.

A few weeks later, I was troubled by excessive bleeding. When I sought the help of the campus doctor, he informed me that it was likely a miscarriage. A wave of mixed emotions washed over me as I heard those words. Despite the positive result on the pregnancy test, the intense cramping and bleeding had led me to believe that I was indeed losing the baby. It was a bitter pill to swallow, but fate had other plans.

Imagine my surprise when I discovered that the night I had sworn him off had resulted in a pregnancy. It was now slipping away from me, but I counted my blessings. At that moment, I couldn't help but think of it as a sign of God's protection. I thought to myself: *It must be a divine intervention that spared me and my child from a future entangled with that man.*

Thanksgiving week arrived, and there I was back at campus doctor. My body ached, nausea clung to me like a shadow, and nothing would stay down. Unbeknownst to me, the news awaiting me would completely catch me off guard - I was still pregnant! I knew deep down that it was the same pregnancy that I had thought I had lost before. In a moment of disbelief, I asked the doctor if my symptoms were due to a stomach virus. His response was filled with a mix of surprise and humor as he quipped, "Umm, the 9-month stomach virus!"

My mind suddenly raced ahead to my upcoming plans! Over the month, I had started seeing another guy, Deon. The next day, I was scheduled to meet his mother for the first time. Time stood still as I grappled with the reality of the situation. How was I going to face him? To make matters worse, he was waiting for me along with his cousin in the waiting room. Thoughts of what excuse to give him to save face in front of his cousin flooded my mind. In a split second, I made a decision and emerged from the doctor's office, mustering a weak smile. "It's just a stomach flu," I lied, "Could you please drop me off? I really need to rest."

Overwhelmed by the unexpected news, I knew I needed someone to confide in, so I urgently requested to be dropped off at a friend's house. Sitting in the car, a wave of emotions swept over me. Of course, the jarring turn of events had left me questioning the future. I started mulling over everything when I was finally dropped off at my friend's house. After all, I was the first in my family to graduate high school without a baby, and I had worked hard to secure my place in college. Yet, here I was, unmarried and pregnant by someone who I knew had no intention of building a future with me.

In the midst of my personal struggles, I met a guy who ignited a spark within me. We shared a deep connection, and the feeling seemed to be mutual. My heart had started to heal from the pain of losing my brother the previous year, and I was slowly emerging from the depths of depression. However, my financial situation was far from stable, and I only had a part-time job to support myself. The weight of responsibility for a child felt overwhelming, to say the least.

With a heavy heart, I made the difficult decision to terminate the pregnancy. Searching for guidance and support, I came across a half-page advertisement in the phone book. "Are you pregnant and confused?" it read. Yep, it resonated with my feelings of uncertainty and the contemplation of abortion. It seemed like the answer I was searching for. Without hesitation, I scheduled an appointment for the end of the week, hoping it would bring some clarity to the tangled web of emotions I had found myself in.

The dreaded day had finally arrived, casting a somber shadow over the chilly November morning. As I stepped out of my car, I noticed the leaves swirling in the wind, creating a carpet of autumn hues. My heart raced with both nervousness and anticipation. I had parked my car a couple of houses down from the location, parallel to the quiet street.

The building before me resembled a house, with a long and slender sidewalk leading to the entrance. It felt as if time stood still. As I approached the doorway, I was in a state of deep emotional turmoil. And then, as if by some strange twist of fate, she appeared before me, seemingly materializing out of thin air. A petite, blonde woman her age, likely in her late 50s, stood there, wrapped in a dark, ankle-length coat.

She approached me with a smile. "You couldn't possibly do what you are thinking about doing if you named that baby," the dark figure stated.

"Excuse me, Ma'am?" I responded, dumbfounded.

She repeated the same phrase, then added with a sense of urgency, "Name that baby right now, so you don't do what you're thinking about doing!"

For a moment, I was speechless. Then, the name occurred to me as if it was sitting on the tip of my tongue. With little hesitation, I yelled, "Justice!"

She smiled, then questioned again, "And what if it's a girl?"

"Justice!" I repeated.

"Good, now you wouldn't hurt Justice, would you?"

Although I simply nodded, her question echoed in my mind. I continued down the long walkway into the clinic's doors. The mysterious incident undoubtedly spooked me, but I remained resolute in my decision to proceed with the appointment.

As I walked into the room, the atmosphere was stark and sterile, characteristic of any typical doctor's office. The sliding window for check-in, gray chairs, and a couple of potted plants scattered around the room did little to alleviate the sense of unease. Generic artwork adorned the walls, devoid of any personal touch or warmth.

Before I could even settle into one of the cold, uninviting chairs after checking in, I was swiftly ushered into an adjacent room for an ultrasound. The sterile environment continued, with the clinical equipment and the dim glow of monitors casting an unnerving glow. I was offered the opportunity to glimpse at the developing embryo on the screen, but I declined without hesitation. How could

I? The thought of witnessing the image of a baby, knowing the weight of the decision I was contemplating, felt unbearable.

After a few quick snapshots were taken and the gestational weeks determined, I was guided into another room. This space offered a slight reprieve from the clinical surroundings, with a large olive green couch and a matching chair positioned across from it. However, even in this room, the air hung heavy with the weight of my decision—that is, until I started taking in my surroundings.

Unbeknownst to me, fate had led me to a place I never expected to be. The room was plain and sterile, typical of a doctor's office, but something felt different. As I sat down on the olive-green couch, I couldn't help but notice the crosses on the wall and the literature about early pregnancy and God's love scattered around the room. It dawned on me that I had walked into a Christian pregnancy center, not the abortion clinic I had intended to visit.

A few minutes later, a counselor entered the room and handed me pictures of my embryo. With tears streaming down my face, I accepted her offer to pray for me. It was a vulnerable moment, and I needed all the support I could get. After the prayer, she gently shared that I was about 10 weeks pregnant. She echoed the words the mysterious woman had told me earlier, "You know, if you named that baby, you wouldn't be able to do what you are thinking about doing."

Trying to hold myself together, I shared with her the encounter I had on my way to the clinic. "A lady approached me on my way here, saying the same thing."

"Well?" she asked, raising her eyebrows.

"I decided to name my baby 'Justice,'" I answered.

She replied, "Well, that's beautiful, but what if it's a girl?"

I replied, "Justice either way."

Her face softened with compassion as she said, "Well, that's beautiful. Justice is a powerful name, whether it's a girl or a boy."

She went on to speak to me about God's unwavering love and how He had a plan for my life. "God is not disappointed in you," she reassured me in a kind voice. She went on to recite Jeremiah 1:5. "Before I formed you in the womb, I knew you," and 29:11, "For I know the plans I have for you," declares the Lord, "plans to prosper you and not to harm you, plans to give you hope and a future."

Her words resonated deeply within me, and I sobbed as she spoke. In that moment, she planted the seeds of faith and destiny that would later bloom in my life. As a token of remembrance, she handed me a small pin with gold feet, symbolizing the size of my baby's feet at 10 weeks gestation. Looking at the charm, something stirred within me. Holding those tiny feet in my hand, I felt an overwhelming love and protectiveness.

"You wouldn't hurt Justice, would you?" she asked gently.

My response was immediate and resolute, "Never!"

In that instant, I knew deep in my heart that I would become a mother. I already felt those maternal instincts. Those little feet touched my soul, and I could never harm the life growing inside me. I pinned the gold feet to the left lapel of my jacket, where they remain to this day. They became a constant reminder—a source of strength and encouragement during moments of doubt.

Leaving the center with pamphlets and vitamins in hand, I embarked on a journey I never thought I would take. I prayed and wrestled with the weight of the responsibility that awaited me. A million doubts plagued my mind. *How can I financially support myself and my child? How will I handle being a single mother?* I just felt unworthy of being a mother. However, in those moments of uncertainty, I turned to that pin, gazing at those little feet, and found solace.

After returning home, I was in a profound state of contemplation. I offered a prayer so heartfelt and full of yearning that I believe it traveled swiftly from my lips to the ears of God Himself. It was a plea born out of love, desperation, and a fierce determination to shape a future for my daughter that surpassed the limitations of my own past.

With every ounce of faith, I possessed, I asked God for four profound blessings. Firstly, I implored that I would be granted the means to give my precious daughter a life far grander than the one I had known. Secondly, I entreated the heavens above that I would not be left to face the daunting challenges of single motherhood alone. Thirdly, I fervently prayed that Justice would never taste the bitterness of growing up without a father's love. And finally, in a moment of vulnerability, I dared to dream that Justice would surpass me in every conceivable way. I yearned for her to rise above the obstacles I had faced.

And lo and behold, God answered each and every one of my prayers. The proof lies within the pages of this very book. For God granted me a remarkable opportunity - a chance to raise Justice in an environment of stability. Mere weeks before I learned of my pregnancy, a man walked into my life, a stranger then, who would become my rock. Against all odds, love blossomed between us. We faced parenthood together as a united front. Deon has been there for Justice since her very first breath, not just a stepdad but a constant source of strength and love. To Justice, he'll always be Dad. I have not been a single mother nor has she been a fatherless child.

When a young woman discovers her unplanned pregnancy, it can feel as though the entire world has been turned upside down. The weight of this realization can be overwhelming, and in those moments, it's important to remember that God has a beautiful plan specifically designed for you. Motherhood, without a doubt, is a journey filled with unparalleled beauty, love, and growth.

In my own life, I found myself at the point of making the most difficult decision I had ever faced. During this moment, a woman – or perhaps I should say, a woman in disguise- crossed my path. Her presence, words of comfort, and unshakeable faith had a life-altering impact on me. That encounter has made me realize that I want to be that guiding light for other women who are terrified and uncertain. I want to remind them that amidst heartbreak, heartache, and confusion, God has a future filled with hope and blessings waiting for them.

Life presents challenges that may initially seem insurmountable, but I've learned that things are never as devastating as they may appear. While I respect that every woman's decision regarding her body is deeply personal and between her and God, I must emphasize that God is faithful and mighty. He can take the broken pieces of our lives and transform them into breathtaking masterpieces. It's crucial not to become consumed by what is currently visible, for things can always improve, even when it seems impossible.

CHAPTER TWO

Perseverance

The disappointment, the exhaustion, the judgment – it all fueled a burning resolve.

Through the journey of motherhood, perseverance is a word I learned to recognize more and more every day. Motherhood is defined by many challenges. It's the bleary-eyed mom, three cups of coffee deep, chasing a mischievous toddler while packing lunches. It's the single mom, working double shifts to ensure every dream has a fighting chance. It's the young mom navigating uncharted territories, learning lullabies, and changing diapers. But it's also the sunshine that smiles after a tearful meltdown, the pure joy of a new discovery shared with wide eyes, and the warmth of tiny arms wrapped around your neck. Motherhood is a paradox – a whirlwind of challenges met with heartwarming determination. It's a constant state of exhaustion punctuated by moments of pure, heart-bursting love. It's a journey that pushes you to your limits yet leaves you forever changed, forever grateful for the privilege of raising little pieces of your heart.

When I took the plunge into motherhood, it felt like leaping into the unknown. There was no clear path, just a jumble of emotions and a healthy dose of fear. So, I know the apprehension of being a single mother. When I started this journey, the anxieties of a single mom echoed in my head – could I do this alone? Luckily, I wasn't alone for long. Looking back, I now realize that I was a single mom mentally longer than I was in reality. I found a partner, but the challenges of being a young mom didn't magically disappear.

College life for most is a whirlwind of late nights, freedom, and maybe a few too many parties. For me, as a young mom, it was a frantic dance between classes, a full-time job, and a screaming baby. The fall of 2006 at FSU was particularly brutal. I was already hanging on by a thread, but that semester took a devastating turn. That summer I had lost a baby at 18 weeks. Although unplanned, I felt grief at losing a pregnancy when I was so close to finding out the gender of the baby. Moreover, that would have been my first child with my now husband. D&C recovery added to the difficulty of my already challenging circumstances. Juggling motherhood and school under those circumstances became impossible. My grades began to slip.

Six weeks after the miscarriage, life took another surprising turn. A faint positive pregnancy test confirmed I was expecting again. This time, it was my son, Deon Jr., and I felt a flicker of hope amidst the chaos. However, the timing couldn't have been worse. Every day, my energy was sapped by morning sickness, which made it a battle just to get to class on time.

As the semester neared its end, another hurdle emerged. Justice came down with a nasty case of croup. The wheezing cough that stole her breath landed us in the hospital for two critical days during finals week. Those forty-eight hours were a frantic scramble. While I sat at Justice's bedside, I felt overwhelmed and anxious. Missed lectures, looming final exams – the pressure was suffocating. However, I knew I had no choice because my baby needed me. Ultimately, I decided catching up on schoolwork would have to wait.

Nevertheless, I tried to come up with a solution. Desperate to salvage the semester, I reached out to my professors by email. I tried to explain the circumstances surrounding my absence in detail. The response was mixed. Two, thankfully, understood my situation. They offered "incomplete" grades, allowing me a chance to make up missed work and exams. Going through the emails, a wave of relief washed over me, but it didn't last long. The rest of the faculty, however, was less forgiving, and failing grades landed on my transcript. With my GPA plummeting, I was dismissed from FSU. I knew getting back wouldn't be easy. However, I gathered hospital records, documented the whirlwind of those weeks, and prepared myself to face a campus administrator head-on.

The meeting with the campus administrator went worse than I even anticipated. When I went up to see him, I was already a bag of nerves, hoping for some semblance of understanding. I vividly remember the look of disgust crossing his face as I appeared in his office with a small child. His cold eyes scanned me, lingering on my belly to notice that I was obviously pregnant again. My carefully rehearsed explanation died in my throat, replaced by a wave of self-consciousness. As I stammered through my plea for readmission, I could sense his unspoken judgment. He continued staring me down, with the same look of disgust, as if I'd been caught in some shameful act. The words that came out of his mouth next shattered my confidence entirely. He spoke with an air of condescension, "You expect me to believe that you are serious about your education, and you sit here before me with a small child and pregnant with another one."

The administrator's words hit me hard, leaving me speechless and reeling. Tears streamed down my face as he spoke, but his voice blurred into a background hum. I couldn't think straight and my mind felt foggy. In that haze, I was unable to process much beyond a fierce determination. Cradling Justice tightly, a single thought pulsed through me: *I have to fix this. I came to FSU for a degree, and I wouldn't leave empty-handed.* A spark ignited within me as I wiped my tears. The disappointment, the exhaustion, the judgment – it all fueled a burning resolve.

His voice finally cut through the fog of humiliation. "Young lady, I am going to give you a chance because of the circumstances," he said with a hint of skepticism in his tone, "but you need to really evaluate if this is really what you want because your actions say the contrary."

Despite the torrent of emotions, I felt a surge of relief wash over me. I mumbled thanks, stood up unsteadily, and exited his office.

Reaching the car, the dam finally broke. I sobbed hard, feeling a flood of emotions I'd held back during the meeting. Disappointment at his judgment, anger at my circumstances, but most of all, relief at the second chance. It wasn't what I had expected, but the turn of events gave me a glimmer of hope.

As the sobs subsided, a steely resolve settled in. I wouldn't fail again. I decided this was my chance to prove myself, not just to the administrator, but to myself. Throughout this crisis, Justice remained my source of motivation.

The next semester constantly challenged my limits, but I clung to that raw determination I felt in the administrator's office. Whenever I felt like giving up, I recalled the memory of holding Justice tight as I fought for a second chance. Every late-night study session and every missed social event fueled my resolve.

Finally, after many sleepless nights, the hard work started paying off. I felt a weight off my chest when I saw my name on the Dean's List. Seeing my name on the list wasn't just a validation of my grades; it was a reflection of my perseverance. It proved that even with a small child, a demanding job, and the challenges of pregnancy, I could excel academically. However, I encountered the most trying time of my college career during my third trimester. Balancing a full-time job, caring for Justice, and a growing belly was a constant struggle. Nonetheless, I somehow found a rhythm and managed to get through. Day in and day out, I was dead tired, but seeing Justice's bright smile and knowing the future I was building for my children kept me going. And against all odds, that semester became my academic peak in college. It wasn't just about achieving good grades or getting a degree. On the contrary, I wanted to prove my strength, my resilience, and most importantly, to myself, that I could be a good mom and simultaneously achieve my goals.

Ultimately, being a mother significantly fueled my willpower. Contrary to how some might view it, motherhood wasn't a burden for me, but a source of immense strength. There's a powerful shift in focus and perseverance that happens when you have a child who relies on you completely. While I've always been capable of overcoming challenges, motherhood took my ability to endure hardship, recover from setbacks, and keep trying to a whole new level.   This strength isn't always understood by others. When they see a single parent struggling, they might misinterpret it as a sign of weakness. In some cases, it can even lead to judgments about my character, with some assuming I'm reckless or irresponsible.

Looking back, that meeting with the campus administrator was just one of countless moments where I had to dig deep for every ounce of resilience. Being a young mother of two meant facing constant judgment – a snide remark here, a disapproving glance there. I often felt discouraged and disappointed. There were days I wanted to melt down, to scream back at the world that felt stacked against me. In these trying times, my faith became my lifeline. It offered solace during those quiet nights battling self-doubt and the ever-present exhaustion. But more than anything, it was Justice & baby in womb who fueled my perseverance. Despite the challenges, I was determined to be the best mom I could be, for Justice, my new baby and for myself.

CHAPTER THREE

Intuition And Advocacy

Our children deserve to be heard and protected.

The journey of parenthood is a continual process of learning, filled with unexpected twists and turns. It pushes you to your limits and challenges you in unexpected ways. Beneath the chaos and the constant barrage of "why?" questions lies a beautiful truth - raising a child is about so much more than just the physical basics. From their emotional well-being to basic needs like food and shelter, everything matters. They're little sponges, soaking up everything around them, from our moods to the way we handle conflict. Amidst their constant chatter, we often fail to realize how they blurt out observations that often go unnoticed by adults. We nod politely, maybe smile, but sometimes those words hold a deeper meaning. They're testing the waters, seeking validation and connection. If we fail to respond appropriately, the children feel unseen, unheard, and neglected. With Justice, I vowed to be different.

Throughout her childhood, I tried to stay closely attuned to her needs by actively listening to her. It's crucial to pick up on subtle cues and emotions to get a glimpse into children's true feelings. Often, these cues go unnoticed by adults focused on their own agendas or are misconstrued as childish whims. But children tend to be quite perceptive. Their anxieties and fears, though sometimes unspoken, can manifest in subtle ways – a change in mood, a lack of enthusiasm, or a seemingly out-of-the-blue outburst. Sometimes, trusting these instincts even means changing your plans. I came to this realization during our summer trip to Florida when Justice's initial excitement about spending time with her extended family turned into a sense of unease.

In the summer of 2008, my boyfriend and I planned a kid-free getaway with friends in South Florida. We figured it was a win-win. Our two kids, Justice was 4 and Deon Jr. 1, at the time would get a fun week with my boyfriend's family in Fort Pierce, and we'd get a much-needed break. An elder of the family, who rarely visited from out of state, was only there for the week, so it seemed like perfect timing. We dropped the kids off with hugs and promises of beach trips. Then, we headed south, looking forward to a few days of uninterrupted adult conversations, poolside lounging, and laughter-filled evenings.

Three days into our kid-free adventure, we were on our way back up the coast, relaxed and sunkissed. We decided to swing by Fort Pierce to see how the kids were doing. We wanted to thank the family for babysitting before continuing to Orlando to enjoy the rest of our kid-free time. We figured it would be a quick visit - a chance to catch up, and then we'd be back on the road.

Our quick pitstop in Fort Pierce wasn't quite as quick as planned. As I hugged Justice Goodbye, she clung to me tightly. "I want to come with you," she mumbled in a small voice.

Initially, I didn't think much of it. I patiently explained to her that it was just a short visit - that she was supposed to stay with her extended family for the rest of the week, but Justice didn't look convinced. She refused to let me go and continued insisting, "But Mom, I really want to come home with you!"

Although I was a little alarmed, I again emphasized that this was her opportunity to spend time with family. "Aren't you having a good time?" I asked gently, hoping to coax out the issue.

Justice's response caught me off-guard. She conveyed to me that she didn't feel as loved as her brother.

It hurt me to hear that. I knew that Deon and I were on one accord of raising our children together as one family. He had taken on the role as father to Justice. We've never used "stepparent" or "half sibling" in our family but we couldn't control how others felt about it. I can imagine what it must have been like for his family to accept the pregnant girlfriend. He had taken on such a huge responsibility at 19 and I had to acknowledge that it may not have been so easy for everyone.

Alarmed, I pressed further. "Has anyone done anything to make you feel that way? Has anyone hurt you? Has anyone mean to you?" "How do you know that?"

"No, but I know," Justice insisted. "I can just tell. She loves Toogie more. "

I was flabbergasted! She was only four years of age, yet she displayed such acute intuition. I double-checked, making sure nothing bad had happened and that no one was being unkind to her. And she confirmed several times that nothing mean had been done to her.

A knot of worry tightened in my stomach. Justice's outburst threw a wrench into our plans. How could I change things without causing a meltdown with the family? I didn't want to make accusations without any rhyme or reason or create a scene. However, I couldn't ignore Justice's clear request. I was in a dilemma; how could I navigate this situation calmly and ensure Justice felt safe and heard?

Swallowing my own discomfort, I went up to my boyfriend and explained the situation. "Hey, babe, we need to take the kids," I stated directly. "Or at least, we need to take Justice because she doesn't want to stay."

Deon looked just as surprised as me. As he questioned me, I told him exactly what Justice had said to me. To my relief, he didn't argue about the matter.

Nodding understandingly, he left to relay the message. As expected, the person was deeply offended by the revelation, and things escalated quickly. An argument erupted between us, leaving everyone in tears. Imagine trying to explain that your four-year-old daughter simply didn't want to stay, stating she didn't feel loved as much as her brother and she wished to go home. Naturally, I was met with cynicism, and I understood. Watching two kids, especially two under 5 is a lot of work. And from a four-year old's perspective, the necessary attention to her one-year-old brother could have made her feel treated differently although she wasn't. It felt like walking a tightrope. While I hated the idea of hurting anyone's feelings, Justice's well-being came first. I did not want to be dismissive of whatever my child was feeling.

That night, the heated argument led to wounded feelings and unresolved conflict. Explaining a four-year-old's intuition was an impossible task, and even in the years to come, the tumultuous night remained etched in my memory. Ultimately, I left that night alongside Justice. The short-term discomfort and hurt feelings were a difficult price to pay, but in my heart, I knew it was the right decision.

There was no evidence that my daughter was mistreated and I believe to this day that she was not. Nonetheless, that day solidified a core principle in our relationship – simply believing her. Even when things didn't make perfect sense, even when logic didn't offer a clear answer, trust in her feelings became a part of the foundation for our bond. It meant listening beyond words, trusting her intuition, and creating a space where she always felt safe enough to speak her truth.

Looking back, that situation showed her, from a young age, that her voice mattered. She saw me take action based on her words, not dismiss them as groundless whining or a tantrum. It wasn't about blind trust, but about validating her feelings and taking them seriously. This became a pattern in my parenting - creating a space where she felt safe to express herself, knowing her words would be heard and her well-being prioritized.

It is my belief that we as parents have to challenge our children to step outside of their immediate feelings but never at the point of questioning their worth or value with others. I knew I'd always protect her, even if it meant going against the world. Taking the kids back during the short visit felt terrible, but the alternative felt more unbearable. The image of Justice's tearful face and the desperation in her voice as she clung to me solidified my resolve.

Now, I realize that true advocacy isn't easy. It's about standing up for someone, even when it's uncomfortable or creates conflict.

That day at my future in-law's house I took a big chance. To offend a member of the family, I wanted to be accepted by was a big risk but as her mother I had to do what was necessary. That was a pivotal moment in our relationship. Believing our children and nurturing their intuition is important. I wouldn't let her be somewhere that made her doubt her worth, even if it meant a strained relationship. Reinforcing soft skills such as intuition, discernment, and courage are critical to development and success in adulthood.

As parents, we have to discern and not be dismissive. When considering what your children are expressing, look deeper. Challenge yourself to consider the long-term implications of your actions or lack of action. What message are you conveying to them? What are you teaching them about boundaries, worth, confidence and communication? When our children express discomfort, it doesn't always have to be a slap or a mean word. Sometimes, it's the little things we might miss - a cold stare, a fake smile, or a stiff hug. These subtle signals can make someone feel uncomfortable, unwelcome, or even discriminated against. Just like a warm touch can make someone feel loved, a cold one can make them feel rejected.

It's a lesson I continue to carry with me – our children deserve to be heard and protected. They need to know that their feelings are valid and that we, as parents, will be their fiercest advocates, even when it's difficult. That's the foundation for a strong relationship and the groundwork for them to become confident, self-assured individuals. When they see us stand up for what's right, even when it's hard, it teaches them the courage to do the same, not just for themselves but for others as well.

CHAPTER FOUR

Sex And Exposure

I felt a wave of guilt wash over me as I realized the unintended consequences of my negligence.

Children's minds are like fertile gardens, brimming with potential and susceptible to whatever is planted within. They learn and adapt at an astonishing rate, taking in information and experiences from their surroundings. This incredible openness is what makes filtering their exposure to the world so important. While we shouldn't completely shield them from reality, unrestricted access to sexual content can be like planting weeds in that fertile ground. These weeds can be difficult to uproot later, potentially leading to inappropriate sexual thoughts. There should be a delicate balance between nurturing a sense of awareness and bombarding them with unnecessary exposure. As their guardians, it's our responsibility to navigate this balance.

Justice wasn't even six yet when I got a reality check on the whole shielding-your-kid thing. My husband and I were in a rough spot, but we were determined to fix things, and more dates seemed like the answer. So, one night, with a sitter booked, I was getting ready for this date night. It felt like a small victory. In the master bathroom mirror, I applied mascara, feeling a flicker of excitement I hadn't felt in a while. Suddenly, a little voice piped up from the bed. Justice, perched there with her usual boundless curiosity, started peppering me with questions about my "plans" for the evening.

"Mom, why are you getting dressed up?" she asked, her curious eyes fixed on me as I stood in front of the mirror, carefully applying the finishing touches to my makeup. I smiled back at her reflection, taking a moment to appreciate her innocent curiosity.

"Daddy is taking me on a date," I replied with a spark of excitement evident in my voice. It had been a while since my husband and I had gone out together; just the two of us. It was a much-needed break from the challenges of parenting and the complexities of our relationship.

"Oh, you're going to go out to eat?" my daughter asked, her eyes widening with interest. I nodded, grateful for her ability to grasp the concept of a date night. She was growing up so quickly, it seemed.

"Yes," I confirmed.

Her next question caught me completely off-guard. "Will you have sex afterwards?" she asked.

I couldn't believe my ears, but the mischievous look on her face told me that I had heard her right. I looked her straight in the eyes, and firmly told her, "Hey, Justice, don't say that word again." When

Justice continued staring at me with wide eyes, I further chided her, "You don't even know what that means, so I don't want to hear that word coming out of your mouth again!"

To my utter surprise, she stubbornly replied, "Yes, I do. I know what it means."

After a few rounds of discussion, I couldn't resist but ask Justice, "Well, what do you think it means?"

She cheekily replied, "It's when two people take off all of their clothes and get in the bed and touch and kiss each other."

I spun around, utterly astonished by her response. It was close enough to the truth, but I hadn't expected her to have such knowledge at her age.

"How do you know that?" I asked, my voice laced with concern.

Justice nonchalantly replied, "I saw it on TV. From Degrassi. It comes on my TV at night."

My shock deepened. I had always assumed that she watched innocent shows on Nick at Nite or Disney channel, never thinking to check what might be playing late at night. I was in utter shock. In that moment, I realized the importance of monitoring the content my child was exposed to. I had unknowingly allowed her innocent eyes to witness something beyond her years. As I processed this newfound knowledge, I made a mental note to be more vigilant in my role as a parent. I would ensure that I provided appropriate and educational content for Justice, shielding her from the adult themes that she was not yet ready to comprehend.

Filled with a mix of shock and concern, I swiftly made my way to Justice's room, determined to uncover the truth about this show she had mentioned. It became my mission over the next couple of nights to dive deep into the episodes, trying to comprehend how such explicit and mature themes could find their way onto a seemingly innocent children's TV station. As I immersed myself in the world of the show, my eyes widened in disbelief. It was a program explicitly designed for teenagers, tackling subjects like sex, teen pregnancy, homosexuality, and bullying with unflinching honesty. The content was pushing boundaries that were far beyond what a young child like Justice should be exposed to.

I felt a wave of guilt wash over me as I realized the unintended consequences of my negligence. In an attempt to provide innocent entertainment for my daughter, I had inadvertently opened the door to a world that was meant for much older audiences. The weight of responsibility bore heavily upon my shoulders as I realized the impact this could have on Justice's understanding of the world.

That incident served as a powerful lesson, teaching me the importance of protecting, validating, and governing my children's exposure to media. From that moment forward, I made a resolute decision to remove televisions from their bedrooms. It became a top priority for me to safeguard their "eye gates," ensuring that they were shielded from potentially harmful content. By centralizing television viewing to common areas, I gained a heightened awareness of what they were watching and could actively monitor and guide their choices.

The realization that Justice had learned about sex at such an early age - only 5 years old, left me with an overwhelming sense of guilt. I had not been diligent enough in validating the content she was exposed to, and she had learned something that did not come from me as her parent. There, I made a personal commitment to be more present and engaged, ensuring that I played an active role in guiding their choices and providing appropriate discussions.

As Justice had already stumbled upon this knowledge, I made the decision to have the "adult talk" with her earlier than anticipated. That night, I took a deep breath and delicately explained to her what sex was, but I made sure to emphasize additional values and principles. I conveyed to her that sex should only occur between adults who were married to each other and that it was intimately connected to the creation of life. I emphasized that only adults who were married and planning to have a baby together should engage in this act. I wanted to instill in her the importance of responsibility, commitment, and the deep emotional connection that should accompany such a profound experience.

I made it clear to Justice that the portrayal of sex she had witnessed on television was far from the reality of the world. When she looked confused, I further explained that those depictions were fictional and often exaggerated, lacking the true depth and significance that should be present in such intimate moments. I wanted her to trust my guidance and know that she could rely on me to provide accurate information and moral guidance. Moreover, I wanted her to know that she could always come to me with questions or concerns, and that I would provide her with honest answers.

It is incredibly important to give our children proper sexual education when they start asking questions, instead of shutting them down. When kids show curiosity about sex or related topics, it's a natural part of their development, and we shouldn't brush it off. If we don't address their questions, they'll go looking for answers elsewhere, and most often, that is not the safest option.

So, instead of avoiding the conversation, we should embrace it. When our children express curiosity about sex, it's an opportunity to create a safe and supportive environment for learning and growth. We can provide age-appropriate explanations, answering their questions in a way that respects their curiosity and aligns with our family values. We also build trust and show them that we're approachable, which encourages them to come to us when they have questions or concerns. Ultimately, by actively engaging in sexual education with our children, we play a vital role in their well-being, promoting healthy relationships and giving them the tools to make informed choices growing into adulthood.

I knew that this conversation was not a one-time event. It was merely the beginning of a story upon which we would build over time. As she grew older and more mature, we would revisit this topic, delving deeper into the nuances of relationships, consent, and personal boundaries. I knew this would be a continuous dialogue that would evolve with her understanding and development.

CHAPTER FIVE

Integrity And Accountability

"Mom, why are you lying to me?"

Anyone who has raised children knows the delightful chaos of their endless curiosity. As you wrestle with bedtime routines, their little voices erupt with wonder: "Where does the sky touch the ground?" "Why are clouds fluffy?" And the perennial favorite, "Where do babies come from?" Explaining these things can be a tightrope walk - both challenging and amusing as they pepper you with their unique perspectives. Some parents might choose the easy way out - a dismissive shrug, a white lie, or even a frustrated scolding. But that path undermines the trust we're trying to build.

When they challenge our answers, it might feel like they're questioning our authority, but it's actually an opportunity. Even as a little girl, Justice showed this to me repeatedly. Due to the circumstances of her birth, there were many situations where honesty and clear communication were crucial. By choosing to address her questions directly, even the tough ones, I learned a valuable lesson: true strength lies in open communication, not in deflection.

As Justice's biological father has never really been a steady presence in her life, I often found myself navigating her questions delicately. There were flashes of effort, times when he'd show up wanting to be a part of her life. But those moments were fleeting. More often than not, it was his parents, Justice's grandparents, who stepped up. Back in Tallahassee, they were always there, and we'd see them all the time. Even when Justice's dad was around, he wouldn't really connect with her. It was like he was just going through the motions, interacting with her but not really engaging. Eventually, Justice had to come to terms with this reality.

During the spring of 2009, Justice came to learn the truth of her genealogy. That time of the year was a whirlwind of activity – the excitement of her first dance recital buzzing in the air, birthday parties for both kids planned for June, and the guest list for these celebrations steadily growing. Family from Tallahassee, ever-present figures in Justice's life, were also planning a visit to join the festivities.

One sunny afternoon, we were all piled into the car - Deon Jr. and Justice bouncing in the back, while my husband and I sat in the front. As we navigated the roads, I rattled off the list of attendees for the recital. "Grandma and Grandpa are coming in from Tallahassee, of course," I said, glancing back at the kids in the rearview mirror. Their faces were a picture of anticipation, especially Justice's, who was eagerly awaiting her big moment on stage. "And," I continued casually, "even your *blood daddy* will be there too."

I could see Justice's expressions change in the reflection of the rearview mirror. She went blank. A frown creased her brow, replaced by a flicker of confusion. We'd always referred to him by his first name.

"My blood daddy?" she repeated the two words slowly, her voice laced with a hint of uncertainty.

I exchanged a glance with my husband as Justice's face scrunched up in confusion. The realization seemed to dawn on her all at once – the friendly man she visited at her grandparents' house wasn't just some nice acquaintance' he was her biological father.

Taking a deep breath, I tried to unpack this complex truth for her young mind. "Sweetie," I began gently, "remember how you were already growing inside me before I met Daddy Deon?" I used the nickname she affectionately called my husband.

The term "birth father" was clearly a new concept for her. She'd always known my husband by his first name, and the distinction seemed to throw her off completely.

Before I could launch into a full explanation, a voice piped up from the back seat. It was Deon Jr., our almost-three-year-old, who'd been intently listening to the conversation. "Wait!" he exclaimed, his brow furrowed in concentration. "Justice gets two daddies? That's not fair!"

My husband and I exchanged a surprised look. Deon Jr.'s innocent outburst, while completely out of the blue, was undeniably adorable. We bit our lips, trying to hold back laughter.

In that moment, a wave of emotions washed over me. Did I just drop a bombshell on my five-year-old? My stomach lurched at the thought. Then came the unexpected twist – my two-year-old's jealousy of Justice having "two daddies." I couldn't help the feeling of self-doubt as I pondered over my way of parenting. How could I have missed this? She knew her grandparents as his parents, yet the connection hadn't clicked. Maybe, I hoped, it was because God shielded her from feeling a gap. My husband had been such a constant, loving presence that she never needed or questioned having a *biological dad*. He'd always been there. Just as her biological father hadn't been present, it seemed she hadn't noticed him much either. But the responsibility to explain everything now fell squarely on my shoulders.

The great awakening within Justice had ignited a newfound curiosity that couldn't be quelled. It was on the following day, as we were on our way back home from school, that she mustered the courage to pose a question that had been brewing within her young mind. "Mom, are you married?" she inquired, her voice tinged with a mixture of innocence and intrigue.

Time seemed to stand still as I grappled with the weight of her inquiry. Finally, I mustered a response, the words escaping my lips slowly and deliberately, "No."

Yet, even as I said the word, I could sense the wheels turning in Justice's mind, connecting the dots that I had hoped would remain separate. "But you told me you had to be married in order to have kids, and you and daddy aren't married," she pointed out, her observation ringing with undeniable truth.

A wave of realization washed over me, leaving me momentarily frozen in my tracks. How had I underestimated her ability to piece together the puzzle of our unconventional family dynamic? And then, without missing a beat, Justice delved deeper into her line of questioning. "So, you can have sex without being married, right? And have kids?" Her words tumbled forth, pushing me into a corner.

Her innocent inquiry took an unexpected turn as she drew a connection between my previous explanation and the impending arrival of my sixteen-year-old sister's child. "And you said that kids can't have babies, but isn't Auntie Nobie a kid?" she asked, referencing the baby shower we had attended recently.

I was completely dumbfounded. I hesitated, grappling with how to navigate this delicate terrain. Finally, I responded cautiously, "Yes. Well, she's a kid, and she isn't married, so she had to have sex. So, kids can have sex and have babies too."

In that moment, Justice's gaze bore into me, her eyes silently demanding an explanation for the inconsistencies in my past statements. It's as if she was asking, "Mom, why are you lying to me?" She was not about to let me off the hook without addressing the confusion plaguing her mind.

Summoning my humility, I met her gaze and acknowledged her observation. "Justice, you are right," I admitted. "Mommy shouldn't have told you that it wasn't possible or even that it was a bad thing. I thought you were too young to understand, so I resorted to simplifying my explanations. But the truth is, there are different ways to approach things - good, better, and best. The best way, as I have always taught you, is for adults to get married before having sex and children. But it doesn't mean that you are bad if you don't follow that path. I simply want what is best for you."

In that moment of vulnerability and self-reflection, I felt an overwhelming sense of gratitude for my daughter's honesty. This unexpected encounter had become a humbling reminder of the power of genuine communication and the importance of embracing our imperfections in the pursuit of understanding.

In my childhood, it would have been unheard of to question my parents regarding such topics. However, the world felt different when I became a parent. At that moment, I realized the days of unquestioning obedience were gone, replaced by an environment where curiosity was encouraged - at least, that's what I hoped for. I wanted my daughter to feel safe expressing herself and to ask "why" without fear of judgment. Maybe it was a reaction to my own childhood, where certain topics were off-limits, but I craved openness and honesty in our relationship.

This approach felt especially important with Justice as she lived up to her name. She had a natural curiosity, so she was a seeker of truth. Even at a young age, she wouldn't settle for simple answers. She wanted the facts, the "why" behind everything. This specific memory lingered with me because she had unknowingly challenged something I said. When she pointed out a flaw in my explanations, I knew she didn't mean to criticize; she genuinely sought understanding.

And so, that day turned out to be a turning point. As I saw her critical thinking abilities develop, I realized how mature she was for her age. Right there, I made a promise to myself – to always be honest with her - to answer her questions truthfully and thoroughly. There would be no sugarcoating, no dodging the truth. I knew it wouldn't always be easy, but it felt crucial to build a foundation of trust.

One of the biggest lessons I learned early on in motherhood is that you're not just raising children, you're shaping future adults. The tender years are when we lay the groundwork for good character, self-worth, confidence, and the crucial ability to respectfully challenge authority. By encouraging them to question me in a safe space at home, I equip them with the courage to navigate the complexities of the outside world. They'll learn to discern truth from manipulation, to stand up for what they believe in, and to be the kind of leaders who inspire others rather than blindly follow the crowd. As Proverbs 21:3

reminds us, "To do what is right and just is more acceptable to the Lord than sacrifice." Raising children with strong moral compasses and the courage to stand by them – that's a sacrifice I'm more than willing to make.

CHAPTER SIX

Coping With Death And Loss

Death is a constant companion to life.

When is it too soon to expose a child to the horrors of death? It's a question that lingers in the minds of many parents. They want to maintain the delicate balance between protecting their innocence and preparing them for the harsh realities of life. Some children, unfortunate as it may be, are thrust into a world of abuse, torture, hunger, and war from an early age. Their childhoods are stolen from them, leaving them scarred and broken. I had grown up in the type of inner-city environment that I never wanted for my kids so shielding my children from such horrors became a priority. The question remains: when is it too soon?

As a devoted mother, I felt a similar way towards Justice. My heart resonated with her every emotion. Whenever she stumbled and scraped her knee, I winced at the pain she must have felt. Whenever she had trouble falling asleep, I tossed and turned in bed, worrying about her endlessly. And when tears streamed down her cheeks, my eyes welled up in empathy. But amidst it all, when her radiant smile illuminated the room, I always felt a burst of joy, which is unparalleled to any feeling in the world. Naturally, I wanted to protect that smile from any harm that might come her way.

Unfortunately, things rarely ever go according to our will. While it is our innate instinct to protect our children from adversity, life has a way of presenting them with unexpected difficulties. These challenges can come in many forms, and even the most well-laid plans may not fully prepare them for every situation. This is an inevitable part of growing up. As children mature, they will encounter experiences that might be complex, upsetting, or simply different from what they're accustomed to. While potentially challenging, these encounters are crucial for developing resilience.

The spring of 2011 marked a pivotal moment in her life as it was the first time she encountered the death of someone close to her. At the age of six, she had been a member of Happy Angel's Dance Studio for a little over a year. It was more than an afterschool program, it was a place of joy, laughter, and dreams in the Publix shopping center near our house. Justice thrived in that environment. The friendly instructors nurtured her creativity, and her rapport with fellow dancers blossomed into genuine friendships. It was a second home - a place where she could express herself freely through movement. My daughter loved going there, until a tragedy struck that shattered the studio's vibrant atmosphere, forever changing the carefree innocence of her young life.

The studio was owned by a beautiful woman named Fabiana, whose life was dreadfully cut short. Fabiana's passion for dance was infectious. She wasn't just the owner of Happy Angel's; she poured her heart and soul into the studio, creating a nurturing environment where students could develop their talents. Justice thrived under Fabiana's tutelage, and her confidence was boosted with every mastered routine. Fabiana's sweet and kind nature had sparked Justice's interest in the art of dancing, igniting a passion that would shape her future. However, fate had other plans.

Things took a horrible turn in ways no one saw coming. Fabiana's life was taken from her at the hands of her abusive husband in a devastating murder-suicide. The news spread like wildfire through the close-knit community of the dance studio. Parents were heartbroken for Fabiana and fearful for their own children as they struggled to explain the incomprehensible act of violence. The once joyful atmosphere of Happy Angel's Dance Studio was replaced by a heavy silence, punctuated only by hushed whispers and tearful goodbyes. As Fabiana fought to escape the clutches of her tormentor, she unknowingly left behind a void in the hearts of not only her own children but also the young dancers she had nurtured. I will forever be saddened by the fact that her desire for freedom from her abuser cost her life.

My heart ached for Fabiana's children, who had their world shattered. Having children of my own, I couldn't begin to comprehend the unimaginable pain they must have been experiencing. Fabiana was a mother just like me, but she was gone too soon – taken away from her four kids, who ranged in age from a curious seven-year-old to a young woman on the cusp of adulthood at seventeen. Being a mother, my heart ached at the thought of what would happen to her children?

Furthermore, I felt a deeper, more profound sense of sorrow for Fabiana herself. What torment, what unimaginable suffering must she have endured at the hands of this abusive man while showing up for others each day as if everything was ok.

Explaining the concept of death to my own young child was an equally daunting task. How does one break it to their five -year-old that their dance instructor was murdered by her husband? In the days that followed Fabiana's passing, Justice struggled to comprehend the magnitude of the tragedy that had befallen. Now, I realize that the traumatic event was indeed a collision of innocence and reality in her life.

As I grappled with the decision of when to address the topic of death, I realized that there was no perfect time. Death is a constant companion to life. Unlike neatly scheduled appointments or meticulously planned events, death doesn't adhere to human calendars or wait for opportune moments. It seeps into our lives when we least expect it as a cruel reminder of life's impermanence.

Dreading the conversation, I knew I couldn't shield Justice from the truth any longer. I wanted her to grow stronger from the experience. I encouraged Justice to talk about her feelings and to express her confusion and grief, hoping that by opening a dialogue, we could navigate this difficult path together. I knew that coming to terms with the truth, as painful as it might be, was the first step on the path to healing.

In the aftermath of Fabiana's passing, Justice's understanding of the world shifted. She learned that life is a fragile blend of both beauty and tragedy. She discovered the strength within herself to confront the harsh realities that exist beyond the safety of her childhood cocoon. She gently cried at her memorial service. Shortly after, she learned of the passing of Michael Jackson on the radio. She wept for him too. It is as if she was formally introduced to grieving. I gave her the space to openly cry and ask as many questions as she wanted.

In the end, I've realized that there is no definitive answer to the question of when it is too soon to expose a child to the horrors of death. It's a balancing act - a tightrope walk between shielding them from harsh realities and allowing them the space to process difficult emotions. Each child is unique, with their own emotional maturity and capacity for understanding. What might traumatize one child could spark curiosity and thoughtful questions in another. Similarly, each situation calls for a delicate balance of love, honesty, and guidance. There's no one-size-fits-all approach.

As parents, we must learn to traverse through these uncertain waters, trusting our instincts and relying on our knowledge of our children. Sometimes, this might mean seeking guidance from professionals trained in childhood grief or having frequent one-on-one conversations with our children. Ultimately, our goal is to provide the support our children need to navigate the complexities of life, including the inevitable encounters with loss. By fostering open communication and offering a safe space for expression, we can help them build resilience and develop the coping mechanisms they'll need to face future challenges. The journey through grief will be unique for each child, but by walking alongside them, offering unwavering love, and providing honest answers to their questions, we can guide them towards healing and a renewed sense of hope.

CHAPTER SEVEN

Leadership A Child Can Lead The Way

It was time to nurture the seed that had been sown and follow her on this beautiful and new journey.

By 2011, Deon and I had reached a crossroads. We had experienced the hardships that come along with growing up together and were at a real "all or nothing" moment. As I matured and mothered a child that was curious and comfortable challenging, I became more convicted about the way I was living and the standard I was trying to model for my children. Deon and I decided to recommit our lives spiritually and the idea of marriage wasn't a hesitant whisper anymore; it was a joyous melody, swelling in our hearts and practically humming in the air around us. We'd been together since that fateful meeting in 2003, and our lives had been a whirlwind of exciting trials and tribulations as we were young and raising two children. We'd built a beautiful little family. Uprooting ourselves from the familiar comfort of our college town was a nerve-wracking leap, but the sunshine of Orlando, Florida, allured us with the promise of new beginnings.

But amidst the whirlwind of "adulting," a quieter yearning began to tug at our hearts, a persistent feeling that something was missing. We felt a growing need to reconnect with our faith to ensure the foundation of our relationship was built on the most solid ground imaginable- ground sanctified by the presence of God. The question of "where" became our constant mantra as we started a heartfelt journey to find the spiritual home we craved. We wandered through the open doors of various churches, and each one offered a glimpse into a different way of worshiping and a different path to connect with the divine. We felt hope flicker with each visit, but a sense of incompleteness lingered.

Finally, a sense of warm yet unexpected homecoming washed over us as we stepped into a particular church in Orlando. It wasn't an ordinary church—rather, it was a place deeply ingrained in my family's past. I soon learned that this was a church that my great-grandmother had attended in her youth. It was as though I had returned, reconnected not only with a spiritual community but also with the generations who had preceded me. This strong heritage gave me a sense of identity, as well as warmth and peace.

With its rich history and legacy, this church exuded serenity and offered a safe haven for our expanding family. It was a place where we could support one another's beliefs and teach our children the value of leading a life characterized by love, compassion, and a sense of belonging to something greater than ourselves.

A seed had been planted in Justice's heart during those church services. While the full weight of the decision might have been beyond her young mind, the sincerity of those who walked the aisle to join the church resonated with her. Their joy, their newfound connection with something bigger than themselves - it sparked curiosity within her and a yearning for something similar.

We continued attending services, and each week, Justice's fascination grew. She'd clap along with unrestrained enthusiasm during praise and worship, her bright eyes wide with wonder. The pastor's sermons, though perhaps not fully grasped by her, held her attention. There was a magnetism in his voice, a sincerity that transcended age. But it was the altar call for others to give their lives to Christ that truly captivated her.

The sight of people walking down the aisle, their faces etched with a mix of determination and newfound peace, filled her with a strange sense of longing. Each person who made that walk ignited a question in her big brown eyes, a silent plea directed towards me. "Can I go too?" she'd finally whispered one Sunday, her voice barely above a murmur.

My heart ached with a beautiful mixture of emotions. There was a surge of pride, witnessing the tender shoots of faith blossoming in my child. But with that came a wave of responsibility. How do you explain the weight of salvation to a little one? How do you convey the depth of a decision that would impact her entire life?

I knelt beside her on the pew, gently explaining the significance of that walk. I told her it meant believing in Jesus, the Son of God, who died for our sins and rose again. It meant a lifelong commitment to follow His teachings and to walk in His light. Her brow furrowed in concentration as she absorbed my words. A flicker of doubt crossed her face; perhaps a sense of the gravity of the situation finally dawned on her.

"That's a big decision, sweetheart," I said softly, squeezing her hand. "It's something you need to think about long and hard."

Justice, ever the thoughtful child, simply nodded. She didn't push the issue, but the question lingered in her mind. It was a decision I wouldn't pressure her into, but one I would wholeheartedly support whenever she was ready.

The following Sunday unfolded in a familiar rhythm. Justice's infectious energy filled the pew as she clapped along during praise and worship, her eyes sparkling with joy. Next, the pastor's sermon took place and while the intricacies might have been lost on her young mind, she sat patiently, captivated by the sincerity in his voice. But as always, her focus sharpened during the alter call.

Her gaze darted towards the front of the church, where people began to make their way down the aisle. Each step they took seemed to echo in the silence. Justice was perched on the edge of the pew, her tiny body barely containing her anticipation. Finally, she turned to me, her eyes wide with a question that mirrored the one she'd whispered the week before.

"Mommy, I want to be baptized," she pleaded, her voice barely a whisper. "Can I please go down?"

My heart clenched with a wave of conflicting emotions. There was a surge of pride - a mother's joy at witnessing her child's innocent yearning for faith. But along with it came a pang of concern. Baptism was a significant step, a public declaration of belief. Was she truly ready for that weight?

"Justice, sweetheart," I began, trying to choose my words carefully. "Baptism is when they put you in water and dip you under to show that you're new because of your belief in Jesus. It's a very important decision."

Her face fell a little. I could see a flicker of disappointment clouding her bright eyes. I reached for her hand, squeezing it gently. "I think you might be a little young to fully understand what that means," I explained softly. "Maybe we can talk about it some more at home?"

Justice simply nodded. She didn't protest or push the issue further, but the disappointment lingered in her eyes. A silent understanding passed between us. This wasn't a rejection, but a postponement. I wanted to give her some time, so her faith could mature alongside her understanding.

The next Sunday, however, the familiar routine took an unexpected turn. Justice remained attentive during the service, and I could sense her growing anticipation. When the benediction arrived, she didn't hesitate. As if propelled by an invisible force, she jumped from her seat. Her small hand shot up, reaching for mine, and she leaned in close.

"Mommy," she pleaded, her eyes searching mine with a newfound intensity. "I want to be a part of the St. John family, please!" she blurted out loud.

I was taken aback by the raw emotion in her voice. Her need to become a part of something greater than herself went beyond just her desire to get baptized. I realized then that my hesitation could not deter her from pursuing her growing faith. It was time to nurture the seed that had been sown and follow her on this beautiful and new journey.

Deon and I exchanged a glance, and a silent conversation passed between us. In his eyes, I saw a reflection of the emotions swirling within me - a potent mix of awe and trepidation. "Babe," I whispered, my voice thick with emotion, "I think it's time."

Deon nodded and his silent support was a source of strength. A smile, shaky yet genuine, crept across my face. "Okay, Justice," I said, my voice barely above a whisper.

Before we could even rise from the pew, a blur of motion shot down the aisle. Justice, fueled by a steadfast determination, was already racing towards the front of the church. A wave of laughter, tinged with astonishment, bubbled up within me. This tiny human, this beautiful daughter of mine, was leading the way. It was a scene straight out of scripture, a living testament to Isaiah 11:6 - a child leading the way.

Deon and I scrambled to follow, our hearts swelling with a mixture of pride and nervous excitement. We arrived at the front just as Justice reached the altar, her small hand outstretched towards the waiting pastor.

Witnessing her stand there, so brave and resolute in her faith, tears welled up in my eyes. It was a moment of profound transformation, not just for Justice but for our entire family. We were joining a new church family, a community built on shared beliefs and a love for God.

The pastor, a kind man with a gentle smile, began his question. "Justice," he asked, his voice warm and inviting, "do you believe that Jesus is the Son of God?"

Her answer was a resounding "Yes!" delivered with a conviction that shook the very foundation of my being. Each subsequent question - His death and resurrection, accepting Him as her Savior - was met with the same unwavering affirmation.

Deon and I stood there, hands clasped tightly together, our hearts bursting with pride. This wasn't just a declaration of faith; it was a declaration of her independence, a blossoming of her own unique connection with God.

The service concluded, and Justice practically skipped with delight. Joy radiated from her in waves. She was no longer just a participant; she was officially a part of this new family. This feeling probably filled her with an infectious sense of belonging.

Later that month, her baptism day arrived. Anticipation crackled around her like static electricity. As she walked towards the baptismal pool, a nervous giggle escaped her lips.

A grin spread across her face as she followed the pastor's instructions. The moment of immersion was a blur of excited shrieks and joyful tears. But when she emerged, her face slick with water, she held a look of pure exhilaration.

Justice's faith journey was just beginning, and I was filled with a deep conviction that I would accompany her on this journey. It was a road we would travel together. Justice's existence was a living example of the transformative power of God's love and the strength of faith.

Her pure spirit led our entire family back to our spiritual journey, and it was more than just a symbol of her own growing faith. A feeling of reawakening pervaded the air - a reunion with something greater than ourselves that had been absent for far too long. Deon and I felt the fire of our own beliefs rekindle when we saw her excitement and sincere desire to join a spiritual community. We began to see the church through her innocent eyes - a place not just of worship but of belonging and acceptance.

Each service we attended resonated with us on a deeper level. The pastor's messages seemed to arrive at precisely the moments we needed them most, offering solace, guidance, and a fresh perspective on the challenges we faced. We knew deep down that we would eventually find ourselves officially joining this church family.

There were practicalities to consider, of course. The 30-minute drive wasn't exactly ideal, especially with young children. Yet, the transformation we were experiencing - the shift in our worldview - kept us coming back for more. We were hesitant about the commitment—the time it would take, the responsibility of being actively involved. But witnessing Justice's enthusiasm outweighed any reservations we might have had.

The decision to join wasn't a sudden one; it was the culmination of these emotions. We saw the positive impact on Justice, the way her faith was blossoming, and it mirrored a yearning that had been growing within us as well. The church, with its warm embrace and a sense of community, offered a safe haven.

So, with hearts brimming with newfound hope, we took the leap. Justice had become a catalyst, a soft prod that brought each of us back to a state of spiritual fulfillment through her tenacity and unshakable faith. It served as a reminder that sometimes, the best leaders are the ones who simply follow their heart, and it was a reflection of the power of a child's innocence. Following her lead, led to our reconnection back to God, a year of abstaining as we counseled before marrying a year later and conceiving our third child, Dorian, on our wedding night in March of 2012.

My message to anyone who is reading this is to recognize, support, and celebrate instances when your children exhibit decisiveness and leadership skills, reinforce their confidence and nurture their potential.

∽

CHAPTER EIGHT

Forgiveness

"You know grown-ups make mistakes, too. I forgive her."

The summer of 2013 marked a significant milestone in my life. It was the time when I eagerly took on the responsibility of planning a mini-family reunion cruise with my in-laws. After officially becoming an in-law following my wedding to Deon in the spring of 2012, I was enthusiastic about supporting the family in helping to organize a memorable gathering. I approached the planning with meticulous care, aiming to create an experience that was both well-thought-out and relaxing for everyone involved. The idea of the younger generation taking over the reunion planning had been discussed within the family, and I wanted to ensure this event lived up to the high standards set by previous reunions. I poured my heart into every detail, hoping to blend tradition with a fresh perspective and make our time together truly special.

Deon's family had always been intentional about gathering with events that were well-organized, filled with an abundance of food and enriched with good conversation and fun. It was critical for me to deliver a consistent experience. Justice was my little helper who assisted me in preparing goodie bags for the family, organizing a cocktail and ice cream party, and cutting out contact cards with room numbers for our entire party. The reunion was off to a promising start. This was the third cruise for Justice and Deon Jr. but the first for our third child, Dorian, who had been born in late 2012 after being conceived on our wedding night earlier that year.

Upon boarding the boat, preparations were made to ensure the kids were ready for the vacation. A routine had been developed for the kids when cruising: exploring the map near the elevators, counting the doors from the elevator to the room, familiarizing themselves with the kids club, attaching lanyards with their room keys, and discussing the importance of not wandering off or leaning against rails. On the first evening, a special briefing for parents with children attending the camp was held. The process for checking kids in and out was reviewed. Justice would be in the 8-10 year-olds group, Deon Jr. in the 5-7 year-olds group, and baby Dorian would remain with us as he was too young for childcare.

One aspect of the camp meeting that stood out was the policy regarding children getting sick. If a child vomited while at camp, they would not be allowed to return for the remainder of the cruise. Justice had already complained of a bellyache just a few hours into the trip, which worried me. If she threw up at camp, she would lose her camp privileges, and there would go my child-free time. To mitigate this risk, I devised a plan. Justice was given the ability to sign in and out of camp, and we went to the nearest restroom to the camp room.

"If you feel like you have to throw up, ask them to call me and sign out and then I'll meet you in this restroom. Okay?" I explained to her.

It was less than 30 feet away from the camp door.

"This way, you don't throw up in front of them and lose privileges to camp for the rest of the trip."

"Okay, Mom." Justice agreed.

And thankfully, she didn't throw up that night as well.

The first two days of the cruise went smoothly and by the third day, we were dreading the end of the trip. On the last night, the kids were eager to go to camp and participate in the after-party, allowing them to stay at camp until 2 a.m. for an additional fee. They were excited about attending and Justice and Deon Jr. begged to stay for all the festivities.

We decided to let them stay so we could have some alone time together. During dinner, they were so anxious that Deon decided to take them to camp between courses.

He returned to dinner and we prepared to enjoy our time exploring the boat. We didn't know that a change of plans was imminent. After attending the 10 p.m. comedy show, we returned to our quiet room to change before heading back out. The room phone rang and a family member on the other end was noticeably upset.

"I need to talk to you." the voice said curtly, "I'm on my way."

A few moments later, a heavy knock was heard at the door. As I opened it, Justice stood in tears. She was ushered into the room, and the person began speaking loudly.

"Do you know what she just did? She took it upon herself to sign out of the camp and start walking around the boat. She had everyone worried because she had left Toogie, and we didn't know where she was." The person said angrily.

The information came in choppy as I heard two voices at once, Justice's voice taking over. She was hyperventilating, and the only words Justice could fully articulate is that she didn't have the right authorization. I was trying to calm both Justice and the person. My husband and I attempted to make sense of the situation.

The person continued, "You need to do something about her being grown and trying to walk around the boat."

I immediately went into defense mode.

"Hey, you're not going to talk to me like that and you're not going to talk about my child like that!" I responded.

The intensity in the small cabin was palpable. My husband stood in front of Justice and me, trying to calm the escalating situation.

Justice finally calmed down enough to explain, "The lady said Dad didn't sign the paperwork for me to stay at the after-party and I didn't have the authorization to make charges to the room. Because I had the permission to sign in and out, they told me I had to sign out and ask a parent to authorize charges to stay."

Justice had come back to the room and didn't find us there. Remembering the contact card she helped to create, she went to different family members' rooms looking for help. When this family member saw her, they believed she had left the camp with other intentions and became worried because they didn't see our son, assuming both had been wandering the boat and that he could have been lost.

"Mom, I promise I didn't try to leave on my own," Justice said.

"I know, I believe you." I replied.

Placing Justice behind me, I defended her fiercely.

"I know my child. If she says that's what happened, then that's what happened." I yelled, the intensity and emotion filling the small space.

My husband set off to the camp to ensure our other child was okay.

At the camp counter, the camp counselor explained, "Dad, you didn't fill out the paperwork correctly. We had to make her leave because she had sign-in and sign-out privileges but no authorization to charge the account. There was a woman here yelling and screaming, and we tried to explain it to her, but she wouldn't listen. And your son is safe."

It was exactly as Justice had stated. Infuriated by all the commotion, I was even more upset that despite the counselor's explanation and confirmation it was an oversight by the parent and not the child's intent, no apology was given to Justice. Instead, more conversation ensued about how we were wrong for giving her the privilege in the first place. No other family members came to our defense or attempted to mediate the situation, leaving me feeling deeply hurt. Despite my efforts to be accepted, I felt truly excluded. Silence in such moments feels like betrayal.

Consumed with anger that night and the next morning, as we prepared for disembarkation, I remember that family member attempting to hug me goodbye. I stood frozen like a statue, gripping my youngest son's stroller, facing forward with my sunglasses on. I had no words for anyone. I only felt disrespected. What stung the most were the statements made about Justice.

In the Black community, it's commonplace to call a little girl "grown." Whenever girls show curiosity, confidence, fearlessness or maturity, they're often reduced to this label. It brought back memories of my own childhood, a term I have always despised. Justice's maturity in handling the situation was dismissed as her being "grown."

People even questioned my parenting for allowing her to sign in and out herself, which was hurtful. I knew my child and what she was capable of. The only reason I let her sign in and out was to prevent her from getting sick and losing her privileges. I wanted to protect her, and I trusted her to handle the responsibility.

My husband spent considerable time having conversations to mend the mess created on the boat. Upon returning to Orlando, the family gathering continued in Fort Pierce for another three days, and the family asked if the kids could still participate.

Before my husband could ask, "Can the kids go?"

I firmly said, "Absolutely not!"

An apology had been issued, but I remained very upset. My husband understood my frustration and he still gently expressed how much it meant for the kids to spend time with his family while they were all there and his words resonated with me and despite my lingering anger, I relented.

"Well, the boys can go, but Justice will not. I'm not going to subject her to anyone who treats her like that."

I prepared myself to have the conversation with Justice to explain why her brothers would be leaving, but she wouldn't. Believe me, it was difficult. We sat together in my bedroom. I took a deep breath and began to explain the situation to her, choosing my words carefully, hoping she would understand.

To my surprise, she asked, "But why can't I go?"

"Well, Justice, I don't want you to be around anyone who will treat you poorly. You don't need to be there. Instead, stay with me." I replied. "Are you not afraid to go?"

"No, she just made a mistake. You know grown-ups make mistakes, too. I forgive her." she said casually. My eyes swelled with tears. Here I was, consumed by anger and hurt while she had already forgiven. There is so much to learn from childlike forgiveness.

I let her go to be with family. How could I hold onto a situation that she had moved on from? I carefully packed up her things, making sure everything she needed was there, and she spent the rest of the week with loved ones. It was hard for me. I wanted her to truly grasp the implications of what had happened, to see how it affected us both.

But in the end, I chose to follow her lead. I let it go because she had let it go. She had the maturity to recognize it was a mistake, and in her eyes, all was forgiven. So, I released my grip on the hurt and confusion, respecting her ability to move past it and embracing the peace that came with her forgiveness.

Watching her ability to forgive reminded me of the importance of letting go, healing, and moving forward with a lighter heart. After one of the angriest moments of my life, I saw the beauty of a forgiving spirit and understood the profound lessons it holds for all of us.

I realized that those opportunities for our children to connect with their relatives were fleeting and valuable. So, I put aside my emotions for the sake of the family, hoping that the time spent together would bring healing and joy.

I am always proud of the fact that I didn't campaign to make her feel differently. Although, I understood the situation differently, I granted her the freedom to follow her own heart.

A love like that described in 1 Corinthians 13:4-7 was displayed—keeping no record of wrongs and holding no grudges, just forgiveness. This experience taught me the power of forgiveness and the resilience of a child's heart. It was a lesson that even in the face of misunderstanding and conflict, love and forgiveness can prevail.

Witnessing such pure and unconditional love reminded me of the importance of grace and compassion in our daily lives. It highlighted how, despite the challenges and miscommunications we might face, embracing a forgiving and loving attitude can heal wounds and strengthen relationships. This profound moment reinforced my belief that true love is about patience, kindness, and an unwavering commitment to understanding and reconciliation.

CHAPTER NINE

Boundaries Within Friendship

"No matter what the relationship or friendship is, if the person does not respect you, then they don't deserve your friendship."

As many parents know, middle school is a crazy time for kids. It's totally different from elementary school. Those years bring a unique set of challenges and transformations for kids. They have to switch between lots of different classes with different teachers who all want different things. Their bodies are changing really fast, which is cool but also kind of weird. And on top of it, their hormones are going haywire, making them feel all sorts of emotions extra strongly. It is often the time when children start to crave independence and begin to craft their own styles.

Justice was no *different*!

Justice was an interesting child with her distinct style. She had a one-of-a-kind style that wasn't about following trends. She had embraced these years with a strong sense of individuality. During this period, she decided to go natural with her hair, reflecting her desire to show off her true self. Additionally, she chose to stop eating red meat, demonstrating her growing awareness of health and personal choices. Her fashion sense was unique, and she favored turtlenecks and oxfords, as I said — never was one to follow trends. She preferred thrifting over shopping at malls, a testament to her independent spirit. She never felt the need to keep up with others, unlike many of her peers, which was a blessing for me. I grew up in an environment where feeling 'poor' was common when you couldn't afford designer things. I had the interesting dynamic of growing up in the hood of Liberty City, Miami, Florida but being schooled in the suburbs of Coral Gables. Being a student that was bussed into a more affluent area gave me a view of both worlds. Although it made me painfully aware of how disadvantaged I was it also gave me a glimpse into a lifestyle to strive for. Justice was able to reap the benefits of being in an environment that nurtured her creativity and not a focus on disparity.

So, after all this, I was surprised when I received a troubling phone call from her school one day.

Justice was in the 6th grade at the time, and she called me choking back tears and a shaking voice, asking to be picked up early from school.

"Justice, calm down. What happened?" I asked, getting up from my desk and rushing to find my purse.

She was choking through her tears and said, "Mom, I just need you to come. I don't understand what I did, but no one is talking to me."

When I arrived at the school, I discovered that some little girl was on a mean-spirited mission and had decided to target Justice. This girl had enlisted others to join her, and they collectively decided to ignore Justice, declaring they would no longer talk to her. No real reason was given, and it was the first time I had seen Justice grapple with viewing herself through the eyes of others.

I honestly felt defenseless at that moment and watching her grapple with the pressure of wanting to fit in and then being abruptly disowned from her friend's group without explanation was heartbreaking. The delicate balance of teaching connection and independence was being tested that day.

Throughout the upbringing of my children, I had always taught them to be friendly, loving and kind companions. They were encouraged to be genuine, polite, cooperative, present, loyal, and trustworthy friends. Until this point, Justice had never experienced a friendship breakup or significant argument with a peer. That day was filled with numerous conversations about friendship. I realized that I had worked hard to teach my children how to be a friend but now it was time to teach them what happens when people aren't being a friend to you.

We discussed the balance of caring about others' perceptions while maintaining boundaries to protect our self-esteem. I strongly emphasized what constitutes a true friend, the importance of mutual respect, and the necessity of protecting emotional well-being. I reminded her that she will always be who God says she is and what she believes about herself. Opinions and Feedback is to make us aware of how others think about us, but it doesn't have to become how we think about ourselves.

In friendships or relationships, it's imperative to establish boundaries that honor our needs and values while also respecting those of others. True friendship thrives on mutual respect, empathy, and support, where both parties feel valued and understood. It's about creating a safe space where we can be authentic and vulnerable without fear of judgment or rejection.

At the same time, it's essential to recognize when certain relationships may be detrimental to our emotional well-being. This might involve setting boundaries to limit interactions with individuals who consistently undermine or disrespect us, even if it means prioritizing our own mental health over maintaining a connection.

Ultimately, cultivating healthy relationships requires a balance of compassion for others and self-care. It's about finding the courage to assert our boundaries while also extending empathy and understanding to those around us. By prioritizing mutual respect and emotional well-being, we can nurture genuine connections that uplift and support us on our journey.

After learning more about the dynamics of Justice's friendship with this girl, it reminded me of a friend from youth. Someone I had spent almost 5 years trying to appease. A friend that required so much attention and would pout and withdraw only for attention and to get me to coddle and appeal to her. Never holding her accountable for her actions or offenses against me. This went on for years before I stood my ground on not being the first one to reconcile or apologize just to move on. We literally never spoke again. I didn't want Justice to fall into the trap of people-pleasing, which will make her empty forever. I made some points clear to her: no matter what the relationship or friendship is, if the person does not respect you, then they don't deserve your friendship. If you don't keep your boundaries, even good friendships can become strained, which will lead to misunderstandings, resentment, and emotional exhaustion.

Anyways, she returned to school the next day, fortified by the love and affirmations of her mother.

"You are loved. You are worthy. You don't have to tolerate mistreatment. Not having you as a friend is a loss to them, not to you." were the words she carried with her.

Although the girls started speaking to her again, the relationship was never the same. Justice was now acutely aware of what they were capable of doing to her. From that moment on, she approached friendships with a different level of confidence and communication. And she is quick to establish what is and isn't acceptable to her. She no longer wasted time with others who didn't value her or showed signs of being poor friends.

The pain and toxicity of unhealthy friendships are often underestimated, especially among women. Justice's journey through this experience provided her with valuable lessons. The importance of setting boundaries in friendships was reinforced. Without them, friendships can become a source of pain rather than support. Her ability to navigate these challenges with resilience was a testament to her strength of character.

Her experience with the mean girl at school was a significant moment that taught her the importance of self-worth and the necessity of surrounding oneself with those who truly value and respect you. It was also an opportunity for me to teach her how to protect herself from toxic behaviors early in life.

CHAPTER TEN

ConfidenceAnd AwarenessIn Identity

"I'm not an Oreo. I'm Black on the inside too.".

In the fall of Justice's 7th-grade year, our family experienced significant changes. After being promoted at work, we had spent about 18 months living in Tallahassee before relocating back to the central Florida market. We moved to Clermont, a town where Justice quickly adapted to her new surroundings and middle school. Despite the challenges that come with changing schools, she embraced the new environment, met friends rapidly, and loved her new school as well. It seemed as though the transition had been seamless for her.

One particular afternoon, as we drove home from school, Justice began recounting the events of her day. Our car rides often went with her stories and experiences of the day, and this day was no different. With a mix of excitement and contemplation, she started to tell me about a conversation she had with a close friend. This friend of hers, a White girl with whom she shared many common interests, had given Justice what she believed was a compliment. Justice explained how her friend had called her an "Oreo," implying that although she appeared to be Black on the outside, she was like a White person on the inside.

Upon hearing this, I instinctively clutched my imaginary pearls and gasped. "So, what did you say?" I asked, curiously and concerned about how Justice had responded to such a comment.

"I told her, I'm not an Oreo. I'm Black on the inside too," she replied confidently.

"Good for you," I said as I felt proud when I heard her words.

Justice went on to explain that she had told her friend, "We have many things in common, but that does not make me more White. We just like the same things despite our different races, but I am very much a Black person," she emphasized.

If I was able to do a slow clap in the car, then I definitely would have done that. My heart swelled with pride in that moment, knowing that Justice had not allowed herself to be "White-washed." Her response showed a level of self-awareness and confidence that few children possess at her age.

Reflecting on my own childhood, I remembered how my friends would sometimes refer to me as a "white girl" when I was her age. At the time, I almost embraced it because I was a victim of the "White is Right" mentality. This mindset made me feel as if being associated with whiteness was somehow better or more desirable. It wasn't until later in life that I began to understand the importance of embracing my true identity and rejecting harmful stereotypes. This realization helped me appreciate the value of my own cultural background and the significance of self-acceptance.

Growing up in the hood, surrounded by poverty, chaos, and violence where everyone looked like me, my thinking had been more contaminated than I realized. To be taunted with differentiation or distinctiveness hadn't seemed like such a bad thing. I lacked the courage and awareness to understand that being called something other than my race wasn't a compliment.

However, Justice had grown up in diverse communities. Although most of her formal education had taken place in predominantly White institutions, her upbringing focused on helping her understand and appreciate herself as a Black woman. It was important for her to see positive and complete representations of Black women, not just the negative ones often shown on TV.

The presence of the Obamas in the White House during her childhood provided a powerful example. She would often ask if she could go and play with Sasha and Malia. Because she traveled often and was exposed to more people who were like her, she showed how comfortable she was with her identity and how easily she fit into different social environments.

I had reached adulthood before reaching this level of confidence and awareness. But she had been consistently reminded and encouraged to be secure within herself, inclusive of others, and keenly aware of how her uniqueness impacted those around her. Understanding that how she showed up in the world mattered was a lesson she embraced fully. It was not about carrying the pressure of being the first or the only, but about recognizing that her presence and influence were significant.

How we perceive ourselves plays a crucial role in how we present ourselves to the world and how others perceive us in return. Our self-image influences every aspect of our lives, from the way we interact with others to the opportunities we pursue. When we have a positive self-concept, we exude confidence and authenticity, which in turn fosters positive connections with those around us.

The importance of self-perception and its impact on how we present ourselves to the world cannot be overstated. Justice's confidence in educating her friend rather than allowing herself to be defined by others was commendable. I hoped that her influence would leave a lasting impression on her friend regarding race and identity.

The opportunity to raise her to know what it is to achieve great things and be Black is not just a responsibility, but an honor. It's a chance to instill in her the resilience and cultural richness that comes with being a Black girl. It means guiding her to recognize and celebrate the achievements of Black people who have paved the way while also encouraging her to carve out her own path of success. It involves teaching her to embrace her culture, to understand the challenges faced by Black communities, and to use her voice and talents to advocate for positive change. Ultimately, it's about empowering her to navigate the world with confidence, strength, and a deep sense of identity, knowing that her heritage is not a limitation but a source of strength and inspiration.

It's important to recognize that some people may refuse to see you the way you want to be seen, and that's okay. That is a "them problem." This reflects more about them than it does about you. It's their issue to deal with, not yours. As parents we must teach our children to focus on being true to themselves and let go of the need for everyone's approval.

As a mother, it was heartening to see Justice grow into a young woman who was not only proud of her identity but also capable of educating others about it. It made me happy to see her understand and embrace that her identity was ongoing, but moments like these reaffirmed that the efforts made were worthwhile.

The experience of raising Justice has been a journey of love, learning, and growth. The values instilled in her—self-respect and confidence in her identity—will undoubtedly guide her as she walks through the complexities of life. Watching her grow and thrive is a source of immense pride and joy, and the journey continues with anticipation for the great things that lie ahead.

CHAPTER ELEVEN

Love And Selection

"As a parent, there is nothing more rewarding than seeing your child navigate the world with confidence and integrity."

As Justice entered her high school years, she continued to grow and flourish. Our household had always fostered open discussions about dating and relationships, and I was determined to approach this aspect of her life with transparency and trust. Unlike some parents who might restrict contact with the opposite sex, I encouraged her to maintain friendships and open communication with friends of any gender.

In middle school, Justice received her first cellphone. I never imposed restrictions on her interactions because I understood that positive interactions with the opposite sex were just as important as avoiding negative ones. My goal was to create an environment where she felt comfortable discussing her relationships openly without fear of judgment or reprisal. I never became a parent who would tell her that she couldn't talk on the phone or befriend those of the opposite sex. I just monitored her phone usage regularly but afforded her the trust to build healthy relationships under my guidance.

Now that Justice was approaching dating age, it became important for her to understand what healthy relationships looked like. I believed that by allowing her to date as a teenager, I could guide her through the complexities of romantic relationships and help her distinguish between positive and negative experiences before she ventured out into the world on her own.

I was wary of imposing strict dating rules or delaying the exploration of relationships until a later age. I had seen firsthand how such restrictions could backfire on those who lacked the necessary experience and understanding to confront the challenges of dating. Some parents have unintentionally harmed their children by imposing strict rules, such as waiting until they're 18 or having moved out before allowing them to date. Unfortunately, this approach can often lead to negative outcomes, especially for young women.

Choosing not to impose such restrictions seemed to have a positive impact on Justice. My own experiences as a teenager had taught me the pitfalls of restrictive parenting when it came to friends of the opposite sex. While I was growing up, my friend David would go by the name Tiffany whenever we communicated. I knew how blocking contact with the opposite sex could lead to secrecy and dishonesty, which were not conducive to healthy development. However, Justice had grown up in an environment of transparency and honesty where she felt comfortable discussing her feelings and experiences openly.

My primary focus was on ensuring that Justice felt comfortable coming to me with any questions or concerns regarding relationships. I wanted her to feel empowered to make informed decisions and to navigate the complexities of relationships with confidence and maturity.

She approached dating with a level-headedness and maturity that belied her years. This, I believe, was partly due to the open and honest conversations we had shared throughout her upbringing.

Around the age of 14, Justice began expressing an interest in dating. While I had initially set the age for dating at 16, I was open to adjusting this based on her maturity level and readiness. About six months before her 15th birthday, as she prepared to enter 9th grade, she approached me with her desire to start dating.

"Mom, I think I'm ready to start dating," she announced one evening.

Surprised but impressed by her maturity, I responded, "Really? Anyone in particular on your mind?"

She shook her head. "No one specific, but I've been thinking about it."

"Well, this is a bit earlier than I expected, but let's discuss it," I said, a smile tugging at the corners of my lips. "I need you to establish a benchmark for your performance. Relationships can be challenging and require a delicate balance between personal life and commitment. Let me know if there's someone you're interested in, but I'd like to observe your performance during your ninth-grade year. If you managed to maintain straight A's in eighth grade, I know that you can uphold that standard." I told her. "Here's what we'll do..."

Over the next few months, we had several discussions about what it meant to be in a relationship and what qualities to look for in a partner. I wanted Justice to understand that relationships required balance and commitment and that her academic performance would serve as a baseline for her readiness to date. Her goal was to be able to date and maintain that baseline. I gave her 3 very specific dating rules that she needed to comply with before going out on a date with anyone.

1. No movie dates: I emphasized the importance of engaging in activities that allowed them to get to know each other better rather than sitting silently in a dark theater.

2. Age verification: I insisted that her date provide identification to verify their age, ensuring that they were age-appropriate and responsible.

3. Proof of responsibility: If her date drove, I requested to see their car registration and insurance, emphasizing the importance of responsibility and safety.

These conversations were important milestones in her journey toward adulthood. They provided her with guidance and support as she navigated the complexities of romantic relationships. More importantly, they reinforced the values of respect, responsibility, and honesty that were central to our family's ethos.

We also discussed the characteristics of a good potential partner. We spoke about the value of dating someone who is kind, generous, slow to anger, willing to listen, and curious. I went as far as describing the observable behaviors of a good young man. He would be someone who is respectful towards women, especially his mother, displays great manners, possibly works a part-time job, and engages others in conversations, to name a few.

We talked about love being the foundation of good relationships, but there are always other factors to consider. I began to share more with her about them.

Our discussions about dating had equipped her with the tools she needed to make informed decisions and navigate the ups and downs of teenage romance.

Justice met her first boyfriend that year, and they are still together more than 3 years later. I like to think that Justice is a "good picker" because she was guided and informed along the way. She was also privileged to have parents who supported and monitored her entry into the dating world.

As a parent, there is nothing more rewarding than seeing your child navigate the world with confidence and integrity. And as she started on this path of her life, I was proud and excited for the journey ahead. With each step, she was becoming the person she was meant to be, and I couldn't wait to see where life would take her.

CHAPTER TWELVE

Mental Health Vs Mental Toughness

"Taking care of your mental health is just as important as taking care of your physical health."

Justice had blossomed into a remarkable young woman during her eleventh and twelfth-grade years. She had become a dual-enrolled student, balancing college classes with high school responsibilities and preparing for life after graduation. Her academic achievements were impressive, with good grades reflecting her dedication and intelligence. Relationships with friends and her boyfriend had flourished, and she managed a part-time job with ease. I noted with pride that she had taken on a leadership position in her favorite school club while managing life during the pandemic with exceptional resilience.

Justice required just a little follow-up after making decisions, which always reminded me of my own high school years. I was also a high achiever in school, successfully balancing my studies, having a boyfriend, and doing a part-time job. She was encouraged to create a strong portfolio of work, aiming for a scholarship that would secure her a freeway into college.

After all these achievements, I couldn't have foreseen that she was somehow suffering. How could I? She appeared to be living just fine. But one evening, while her father and I were watching TV in the living room, she approached us and politely said she wanted to talk.

"Umm... Mom, Dad. I think I need a therapist," she said.

We both exchanged a look of confusion.

"For what, Justice?" we asked curiously.

She explained that she hadn't been feeling quite like herself lately and felt that it was necessary to speak with a professional. We gently suggested that it might simply be performance anxiety from studying for SATs and a packed schedule. We also suggested that she should toughen up and practice gratitude, considering she was more blessed than many. However, she stood her ground and insisted, continuing to seek confidential guidance to sort through her thoughts.

We detected a seriousness in her voice that couldn't be ignored. My initial reaction to her depression was one of surprise. I couldn't help but think about the life she was blessed with—both parents, a two-story comfortable home, her own car, her personal room, and a supportive community of people who cared deeply for her.

I took a step back and reflected on all the times I had suffered mentally despite everything appearing fine on the surface. At that point, I had a nice position at work, a company car, six-figure salary, and I still had moments of unfulfillment and unhappiness. I've struggled with over-achieving, code-switching, and imposter syndrome at different times in my career. I had to realize that no matter how hard I tried, I couldn't protect her from everything.

I felt proud of the courage shown by Justice when she approached us to talk about her feelings. The level of self-awareness it took to know she needed a different level of support. This situation provided an opportunity to explore the delicate balance between mental toughness and addressing mental health, a distinction that may not have been clear to her before. I realized that while some things are taught, others are caught. She had witnessed me consistently overcoming challenges and achieving promotions but had not heard enough about the times I battled through tears, cried privately in showers, or knelt in exhaustion and despair.

This experience facilitated a new level of openness. I shared more of my vulnerabilities with her and allowed her to see that despite my outward strength, there were moments when I faced fear head-on. I've always believed in bending, but breaking should never be an option. I shed tears, and that's natural, but I wipe them away before leaving the room. Failing to strike this balance with vulnerability had created a false, distorted sense of self. She had been too hard on herself for feeling tired, doubting herself, or just feeling down. I cherished her image of me as a superwoman, but it was crucial for her to understand that I was simply a woman who refused to let negative thoughts dominate.

The following week, I dedicated myself to finding her a local counselor. We successfully connected her with a therapist, and she immediately clicked with her. Her sessions opened up deeper conversations between us as mother and daughter. Despite my belief that I hadn't pressured her, she felt it naturally because she simply wanted to make me proud. She was keenly aware of all the sacrifices I had made and earnestly desired for me to recognize that they were not in vain. It was heartbreaking to learn that my child had ever felt that way. I've never wanted any of my children to think that my love for them was conditional on their performance. This prompted a reassessment of how I balance accountability and morale.

I was reflecting on my own childhood memories of my dad visiting town and taking my brother and me to Pizza Hut when we achieved good grades. As a straight-A student for most of my life, it was interesting to consider how innocent rewards like these could instill a lifetime of perfectionism and an insatiable need to excel.

I no longer looked at attendance and grades in the same light. I reward results, but I also recognize efforts. I use grades as a gauge of their mastery and understanding rather than as a determinant of whether we engage in family leisure activities. We made conscious efforts not to promote mediocrity while ensuring the belief that love, time, and attention would not change based on a report card.

Each of my children is unique to me, and I practice situational leadership in raising them. I avoid comparing them to each other and celebrate their accomplishments both individually and collectively. They never have to compete for affection or worry about unequal love based on their performance. This experience with Justice underscored the importance of being mindful of how performance is rewarded and how love and support are expressed.

I strengthen my belief that all parents should consider how they reward achievement, and recognize effort while demonstrating support.

Justice's journey clearly demonstrated how imperative it was to support her mental health needs. This decision not only equipped her with the skills to manage challenges but also deepened our bond. The conversations we had and the experiences we shared during this time served to create a greater understanding and appreciation for each other.

This story represents an emotional reminder of the importance of addressing mental health and cultivating a supportive environment for our children. It emphasizes the necessity of open communication, empathy, and understanding—the resilience gained through vulnerability and the transformative impact of seeking help when it's needed most.

As parents, we shoulder the responsibility of balancing the encouragement of excellence with safeguarding emotional well-being. The significance of prioritizing mental health, practicing self-care, and maintaining open lines of communication cannot be emphasized enough.

CHAPTER THIRTEEN

Our Graduation

"In raising Justice, God raised me."

Justice was just a little six-year-old kid when I first started writing this book. I originally named the book, "Justice Sayings," as I journaled all the interesting things she did and said growing up. Back then, it felt like I was stuck on a hamster wheel, going nowhere fast. No matter how hard I tried, the story wouldn't come together despite my best efforts, like I was constantly circling the same ideas without ever reaching a satisfying conclusion. It feels funny now when I look back! Perhaps the story was simply just waiting for the perfect time to come together.

It was around Spring in 2022 and guess what? My heart was bursting with joy! Justice was walking across the stage at the Clermont Rec Center and she was about to get her Associate's degree. This was all happening just a week before her high school graduation. And she was only seventeen! It felt like a perfect conclusion to her childhood story.

A week later, she was holding her high school diploma and Associate's degree while ready to pursue her dreams at a four-year university. That's why I assumed, "This is where the book ends." But one thing I've learned about God – He's far more creative and glorious than that. There was a graduation in store for me, too.

In September of 2021, I had been hospitalized with Covid followed by 3 months of oxygen treatment. It was probably one of the scariest moments of my life. Sitting in a hospital, away from my family, afraid that I wouldn't make it back home to them was terrifying. I had been so busy with life that the inability to move allowed me to think differently about what was most important to me. It was the beginning of a shift in my mindset. I remember thinking, *If I leave today, have I done all the things I wanted? Have I left my kids with the memories and advice that is important for them to know? Am I operating in my purpose? Am I living the life that God wants me to live?* In many ways, I couldn't answer the questions satisfactorily.

I returned to work after the incident very different. In the quietness of my recovery, I learned the difference between "who I am" and "what I do". I realized how much the work that I was doing in the corporate world had become a part of my identity and that I was limiting my potential with all the things that God called me to be. Realizing that who you are is more than the job that you do is a game changer.

So, as Justice graduated from high school, I began a new journey of discovering what I really wanted the next chapter of my life to look like. I had become intentional about better aligning my work with my purpose. I had received another promotion at work and initiating it felt one step closer to the work I knew I was destined to do. It was a director-level position where I would help in the leadership development of all the managers of a +70k employee company.

Fast forward to 2023, I left my corporate job. My position was eliminated and although offered another role, that work and the environment did not align with my purpose, so I decided to leave and began my journey into full-time entrepreneurship. Over the year, I developed an acute determination to be intentional in living the life I believe God wants for me. Much like the young mother I was 19 years ago, I had to look past my current circumstances and take action, knowing that with faith and hard work, God would answer my prayers like he had done before.

2024 is the year when Justice and I both graduated.

On May 4th, I had the privilege of returning to the city where Justice was born. It was just steps away from the campus where I once walked with her in my belly and I watched her proudly cross the stage to receive her Bachelor of Science in Business. In that moment, all I could think was, "Wow, I am the 19-year-old pregnant girl who raised the 19-year-old college graduate."

It had been exactly twenty years since I carried her in my womb. It felt like yesterday I was holding her tiny hand for the first time, and here she was, walking across the stage as a grown woman. I was emotional, but it wasn't sad feelings. I felt blessed that God allowed me to witness the incredible joy of seeing her graduate at the same age that I was when I carried her. It was a moment more beautiful than anything I could've ever imagined. All the late nights studying, the pep talks, the consistent persistence – it all led to this. Seeing her graduate was more than just her achievement; it was ours.

She was graduating and not like I had. My graduation day was melodramatic, the flu had me feeling like death warmed over; I was exhausted from packing because we were moving to a new city that same weekend and honestly I was just relieved it was finally done. My diploma is still covered in dust somewhere in a box. Don't get me wrong! I was proud of it and finishing college, but I was ready to have a life where I wasn't balancing school, work and motherhood.

Now, I have graduated as a business owner. It was nearly a year since I started running my own business. Coaching and motivating hundreds of leaders on topics of resilience, psychological safety, balancing accountability and morale and more. All topics that feel like I'd been preparing for my whole life. God had equipped me to train others in the very same things that had helped me to be successful over the years.

Justice graduated "magna cum laude," which speaks to her spirit of excellence and hard work. I had managed to ensure Justice would graduate debt-free by paying her remaining tuition after her scholarship award. On top of that, she secured a fellowship grant to help with her graduate studies, gained valuable work experience through maintaining a part-time job and a summer internship, and already had a job lined up after graduation. This meant she could travel and explore if she wanted, but more importantly, she was well-prepared financially and professionally for adulthood. It was an honor to provide an environment that allowed her to relish in her graduation moment.

Now, at the age of nineteen, she doesn't have to figure out this world alone. It's hard to believe how quickly time flies. I'm so proud to see her begin to walk on her path and The best part? I still stand beside her with the utmost support and guidance so she won't have to do it all alone. I'll always be her biggest cheerleader.

Looking back, there were many times of doubt and worrying about life ahead of us. I was afraid of what life might bring but also hopeful—carrying the courage, dedication and grit of hope.

God answered the prayers that I prayed for her while she was in my womb. I've been blessed to have my husband by my side, protecting me from the difficulties of single motherhood. Justice has never known the pain of growing up without a father, as she was fortunate to have a dad who has been there for her since birth. Through God's grace and my hard work she has been provided with a comfortable life where all of her needs and many of her wants were fulfilled. *Finally, God has allowed her to surpass me.*

This has truly been *our graduation*. And I wouldn't trade all these moments for anything in the world. God has created a life filled with challenges, victories, hardships, highs, lows, and achievements. And they all matter. It's amazing that as I was raising Justice, God was raising me.

Acknowledgment

I want to acknowledge a group of people whom I'll forever be grateful for their role in producing this book.

Firstly, Dr. Danielle McKinnon, thank you for your loyalty, dedication, and the seed you sowed into the production of this book. You have been an amazing friend. Our friendship is not a story of perfection but definitely one of progression. Despite my tenacity and can-do attitude, I appreciate that you have been a friend who consistently lightened my burdens. Your support has made challenges easier and ensured that I didn't have to face them alone. I appreciate you for being a great Godmother, and I'll never forget the support you offered when it mattered most – from the delivery room to birthday parties and graduations. Your secret sauce has always been your ability to show up. I love you, my friend.

To Ludny Longchamp, Sherrel Sampson, Cheri Crum, Ashley Still and Danielle Farmer, you were among the first to answer the call—the first members of my book ambassador team. Your support, advice, and friendship throughout this process mean the world to me.

To all my beta readers – Dario S., Tony M., Jodie M., Sheryl W., Xochil E., Kesha T., Marissa L., Wanda M., Jolanda B., Devonya R.,

Tracey M., and Jeff S. – thank you for your invaluable support and feedback. I sincerely appreciate every one of you.

About The Author

DORIS JACKSON SHAZIER IS AN AUTHOR, SPEAKER, AND ICF-ACCREDITED LEADERSHIP COACH WITH OVER TWENTY YEARS OF EXPERIENCE IN DRIVING ORGANIZATIONAL GROWTH AND EXCELLENCE. RENOWNED FOR HER GENUINE AND COLLABORATIVE LEADERSHIP STYLE, DORIS PLAYS MULTIPLE ROLES—AS A LEADER, MENTOR, TRAINER, FACILITATOR, AND PRINCIPAL LEADERSHIP COACH & CONSULTANT AT SHAZIER COACHING & CONSULTING.

DORIS IS THE PROUD WIFE OF DEON AND MOTHER OF JUSTICE, DEON JR., DORIAN, AND DAVION. SHE IS A TRUE FLORIDIAN, HAVING GROWN UP IN MIAMI, FLORIDA, BEFORE ATTENDING COLLEGE IN TALLAHASSEE, FLORIDA, AND NOW RESIDING IN CENTRAL FLORIDA. SHE IS DEEPLY PASSIONATE ABOUT EMPOWERING LEADERS AND FAMILIES THROUGH TEACHING STRATEGIES TO CREATE HIGH-ACCOUNTABILITY, HIGH-MORALE ENVIRONMENTS AT WORK AND HOME.

FIND OUT MORE ABOUT DORIS AND HER MISSION TO DEVELOP GOOD LEADERS IN THE WORKPLACE AND HOME AT DORISJACKSONSHAZIER.COM.

IIF YOU ARE INTERESTED IN LEADERSHIP DEVELOPMENT & COACHING FOR YOURSELF AND/OR YOUR TEAM, CONTACT DORIS AT INFO@DORISJACKSONSHAZIER.COM.